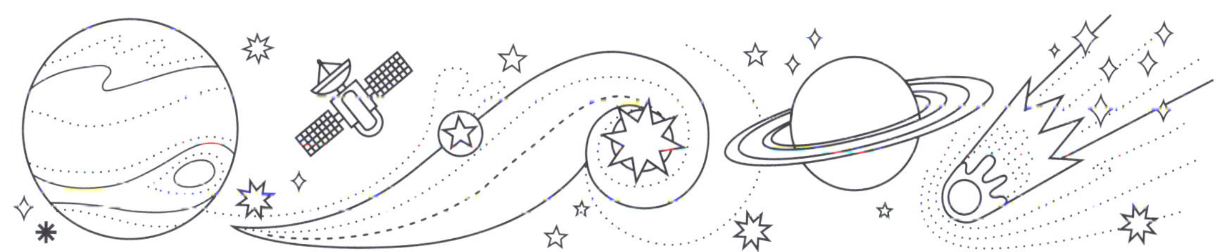

Name

Teacher

School

Learning goal: To improve knowledge of the alphabet in Victorian Modern Cursive script

Success criteria:

- I can write all lower-case and capital letters of the alphabet in Victorian Modern Cursive.
- I can write all lower-case and capital letters of the alphabet in Victorian Modern Cursive legibly, using appropriate slope, spacing and size.

Are you ready to write?

Posture

Ensure your feet are flat on the floor and you are sitting well back in the chair.

Paper position

left-handed

Hold the paper with your non-writing hand.

right-handed

Pencil grip

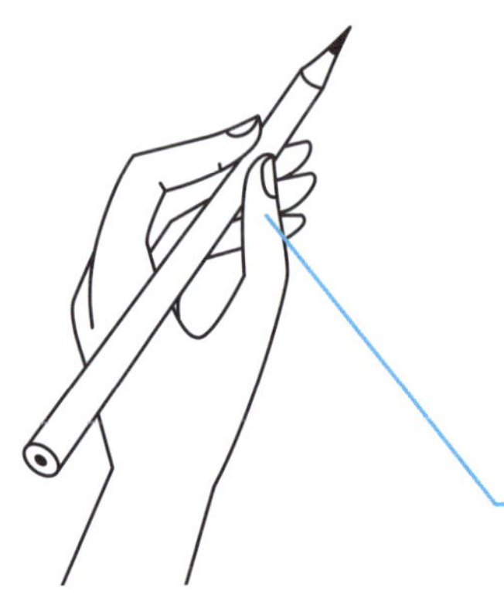

left-handed

Hold your pencil with one finger on top of the barrel.

Support the barrel with your thumb.

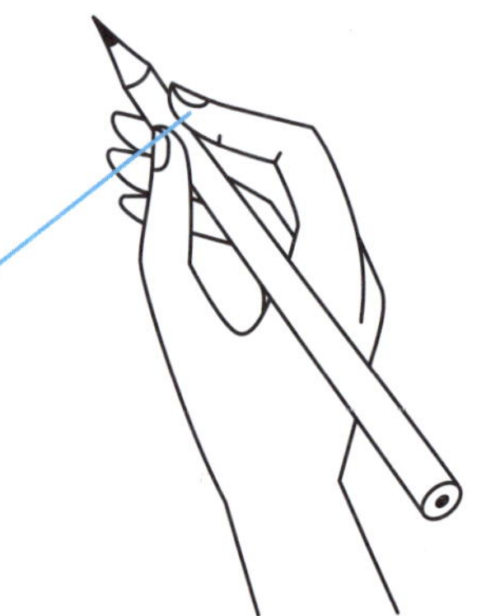

right-handed

Unjoined letters

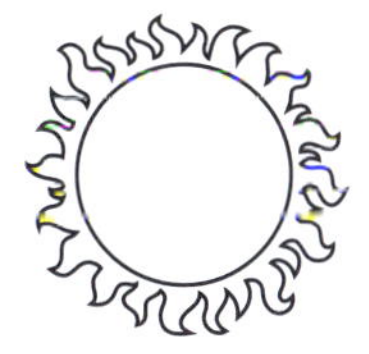

Revise your unjoined letters. Copy the alphabet. Then place a dot at the correct starting point of each letter.

a b c d e f g h i j k l m n o p q r s t u v w x y z

Match each word to its meaning, then copy the text.

Stars	NASA	Orbits

__________ : astronomical bodies that are visible at night and are not planets.

__________ : the paths Earth and other planets take around the Sun.

__________ : the USA space agency that sent the first person to land on the Moon.

ISBN: 9780170424073

Capital letters

Revise your capital letters. Copy these words.

SCIENCE RESEARCH ENERGY

LUNAR UNIVERSE SOLAR

ATMOSPHERE FUSION ECLIPSE

ROTATE GRAVITY AXIS

Rewrite these words in all capital letters.

asteroid radio waves

satellites moon phases

crescent equinox elliptical

transit momentum velocity

Numerals

Revise your numerals. Write the missing numerals in the gaps, then copy the text.

Earth is one hundred and fifty million kilometres from the Sun.

= ________________ *km*

The circumference of Earth is forty thousand and thirty kilometres.

= ________________ *km*

It takes three hundred and sixty-five days for Earth to orbit the Sun.

= ____________ *days*

get.ga/PMWA100

ISBN: 9780170424073

Speed loops from clockwise finishers

galaxy

Using speed loops from the letters g, j, y and z can help you to write faster and with more fluency.

When making a speed loop from g, j, y or z, trail your pen from the end of the letter, crossing at the baseline. The loop should be about half the width of the letter.

go jump yonder zero

loop crosses at the baseline

Copy these letter pairs.

gl ga gu gr gh ge gl ga gu gr

ja ju jo ji je ja ju jo ji je

yl yr yo yu ye yi ya yl yr yo

zl za ze zi zo zu zy zl za ze

mystery

Remember: a speed loop is not needed if g, j, y or z is at the end of a word.

Copy these words with speed loops from 'g'.

gravity age large gust great

grip glisten green grow

grass gory guide gutter

Copy these words with speed loops from 'j'.

jaguar jumped join object

adjust jest jam jig joy

jewels jacket jive justice

Apollo 13 Command Module *Odyssey*

Copy these words with speed loops from 'y'.

year young yes lying yesterday

myriad yacht yoyo yappy yurt

staying yoghurt yippee yummy yak

Copy these words with speed loops from 'z'.

zodiac zip zoom lazy wheeze zoo

zebra zero hazy dizzy zone ooze

blazing sizzle zap jazz fuzz fizz

Copy these words ending in 'z'.

quiz buzz waltz quartz topaz whizz

Speed loops to ascenders

Using speed loops when joining to b, h, k and l makes joining letters faster because there is less to retrace on the downstroke.

magic line

ph ck

Make sure the loop and the ascender meet at the magic line.

Copy these letter pairs with speed loops to ascenders.

rb ib mb ob ub bb lb ch ph gh

sh th oh ch ph ek ok ck nk rk

sk ak ek ok al ol ul pl rl gl

black hole

Remember: a speed loop is not needed if b, h, k or l is at the beginning of a word.

Copy these words with speed loops to ascenders.

suburb bib comb graph wish

tough speak plank girl howl

ISBN: 9780170424073

Rewrite the text in cursive. Remember to use speed loops to ascenders in b, h, k and l correctly.

A black hole is a region in space where the force of gravity is so strong that light is not able to escape. Scientists can locate a black hole by observing its effect on stars and gases around it. The Sun does not have enough mass to become a black hole. At the end of its life, it will become a red giant. It will then burst the outer layers and become a planetary nebula. Finally, all that will be left will be a white dwarf star.

Copy the text, then complete the last three lines of the poem in cursive. Include as many words as you can from the box below.

shower	starburst	blast	planet	
phase	photo	sky	blue	streak

I blink in awe at the beauty of the

constellations above me,

A cluster of brightness in the night,

I think of the astronauts who went

forth like shooting stars,

Full of bravery and optimism,

I wonder

ISBN: 9780170424073

Speed loops to 'f'

dwarf

reflex

Remember: use a speed loop to join horizontally or diagonally to 'f'.

When 'f' is in the middle of a word, use the crossbar to join to the next letter.

Copy these words with joins to 'f'.

beliefs perform unsafe leaf reflex

wonderful afterwards awfully

after loaf ruffle rafter therefore

lift off turf before puff wolf

flare

Remember: when 'f' is at the beginning of a word, it doesn't need a speed loop.

Copy these words with 'f' at the beginning of the word.

flare freeze fumble faint fabric

ISBN: 9780170424073

Practising speed loops in smaller lines

Copy the text to practise speed loops in smaller lines.

Astronomers are very interested in dwarf planets,

which are mostly located in the outer solar system.

In 2015, two NASA space probes visited dwarf planets:

'Dawn' reached Ceres, and 'New Horizons' reached

Pluto. Ceres is located in the asteroid belt. It is so

little that it is classified as both a dwarf planet

and an asteroid. Because dwarf planets are small,

their gravity is not sufficient to attract or push away

smaller bodies. Scientists have long been enthralled

by the effects of gravity. It is a force great enough

to affect the speed of a space shuttle as it lifts off

from Earth and zooms into outer space.

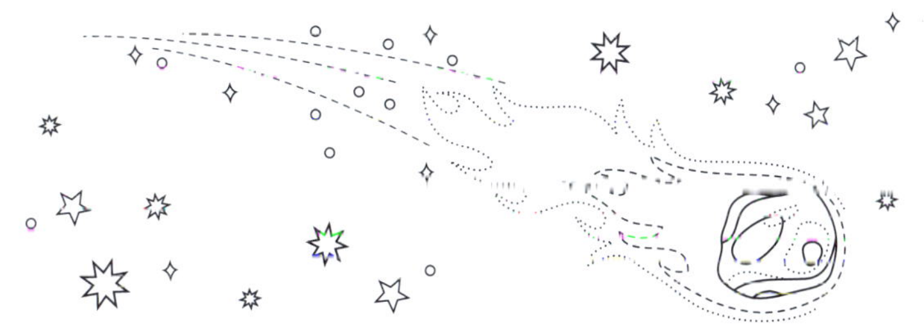

get.ga/PMWA181

ISBN: 9780170424073

Rewrite the text in cursive. Take special care to add speed loops correctly where required.

Neptune is fresco blue in colour and is named after the god of the sea in Roman legend. It is a cold, dark planet with the strongest winds in the solar system. Neptune is one of the gas giants, and the furthest planet from the Sun. Neptune has 13 known moons. It has only been photographed up close once in space history, when the spacecraft Voyager 2 zoomed there to visit.

Peer review

Ask your partner to give you some feedback on how well you wrote the text above. Ask them to notice how carefully you formed your speed loops.

2 stars (two things you did well)

1 wish (a way for you to improve)

Diagonal joins

When making a diagonal join, extend the exit flick of the first letter at a 45° angle to join to the second letter.

Copy these letter pairs with diagonal joins.

am an ap ei em ev in un

ci di hi pi le me ne te

du hu mu nu cy my ty xy

Copy the text. Then underline the diagonal joins.

Infrared telescopes find objects in space by detecting the infrared radiation they emit. They can be used to look through space dust and molecular clouds, so we can see planets. Astronomers also use optical and x-ray telescopes to study our universe. Some telescopes are in observatories on Earth. Others, like the Hubble Space Telescope, are launched into orbit to get a better view of objects in outer space.

Diagonal joins from 'q'

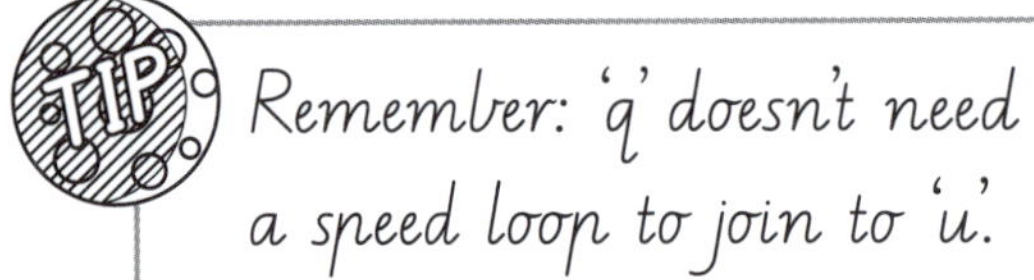

Copy these 'qu' letter pairs.

qu qu qu qu qu qu qu qu

Copy these words with diagonal joins from 'q'.

equinox quad square squid squash aquatic

queen question squat quill equipment quick

quiet equally quarter quench quotation unique

quail squawk quiz quickly squeeze squeak

qualify liquefy squirm quiver quake quilt

Copy the text, being careful with your diagonal joins from 'q'.

Every year there are two equinoxes, when day and night are of equal length. Scientists used to question when the equinoxes would occur. Scientific equipment was also used to research the four phases of the Moon.

get.ga/PMWA182

Diagonal joins from 's'

Speed up your handwriting by retracing along the bottom of the letter 's'.

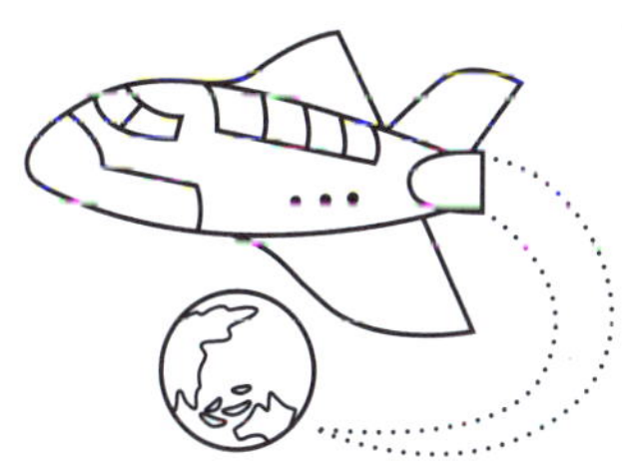

Copy these letter pairs with diagonal joins from 's'.

so sy su sm su sp sh sk sl st so sy

Copy these words with diagonal joins from 's'.

solar system solstice symbol supergiant space

spiral supernova spectrum supercluster surface

storm shower stratosphere shooting star sky

stellar shock study starburst strata stone

astronauts terrestrial protostar exhaust celestial

Copy the text, being careful with your diagonal joins from 's'.

The Commonwealth Scientific and Industrial Research Organisation (CSIRO) is an Australian agency that studies space. It manages observatories that conduct useful radio astronomy research. CSIRO scientists also track spacecrafts on interplanetary missions.

ISBN: 9780170424073

Diagonal joins to 's'

as → as

Remember: when joining diagonally to 's', speed up your handwriting by modifying the shape of your 's' so there is less to retrace.

Copy these letter pairs.

as cs ds es is ks ls ns ps ts us ys

Copy these words with diagonal joins to 's'.

astronomer phase cluster crescent density list

comets dust planets giants Uranus storms

moons skies debris gas sustain suspicious

acclimatise rotates axis pseudo session

weightlessness rays vision luminous system asset

unstable molecules physics historic kilometres

workstation airlocks expulsion hailstone landscape

ISBN: 9780170424073

Diagonal joins and speed loops

When making a diagonal join to an ascender, make sure the loop crosses at the same height as the top of a body letter.

Copy these letter pairs.

ab db eb ib lb mb nb ob ub

ah ch eh ih mh uh ak ck ek ik

lk mk nk ok uk al cl el il ll

ml nl ol af ef if lf mf of uf

Copy these words with speed loops from diagonal joins.

satellite telescope nebula fuel experimental

dock vehicle altitude unstable constellation

stellar theory velocity flight Alpha Centauri

wavelength propellant bellow black hole

electricity rocket technology chart yellow

Hubble Space Telescope shuttle torch shelter

sphere allow think bubble cling abstract

ISBN: 9780170424073

Diagonal joins to 'f'

Remember: when joining to 'f', continue the exit of the letter before and form a loop.

Copy these letter pairs with diagonal joins to 'f'.

af ef if of uf lf mf nf af ef if of uf lf

Copy these words with diagonal joins to 'f'.

lift infrared spacecraft fifteen after

fifth difference lifesaving shelf effect

Write sentences using the words in the box below. Take special care with your joins to 'f'.

spacecraft lift infrared

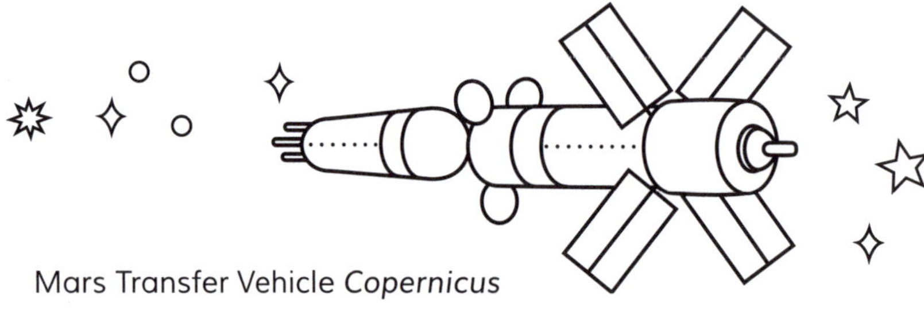

Mars Transfer Vehicle *Copernicus*

Diagonal joins review

Take a letter from each box to make letter pairs with diagonal joins.

nt

a c d e h i k l m n p t u x	to	b e h i k l m n t u y z

Copy the phrases, then underline the diagonal joins.

International Space Station unique place

six people live occupied since November 2000

conduct research solar arrays provide power

inside a laboratory contains observatory module

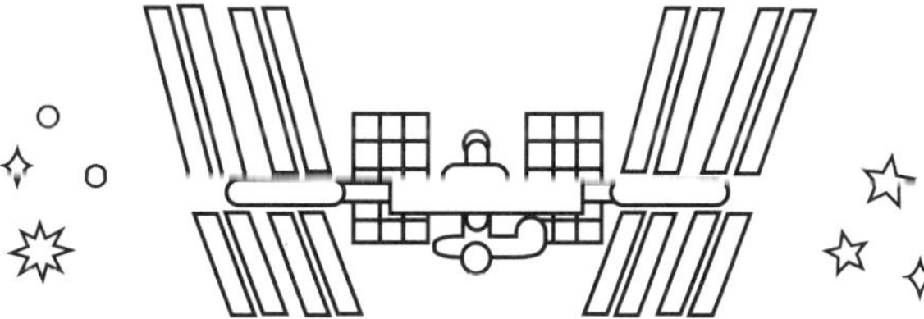

get.ga/PMWA183

Make new words by adding a letter or letters to these word endings with diagonal joins.

_______ake _______ain _______ate _______ill

_______ait _______ail _______ink _______ent

ISBN: 9780170424073

Self-assessment: Diagonal joins

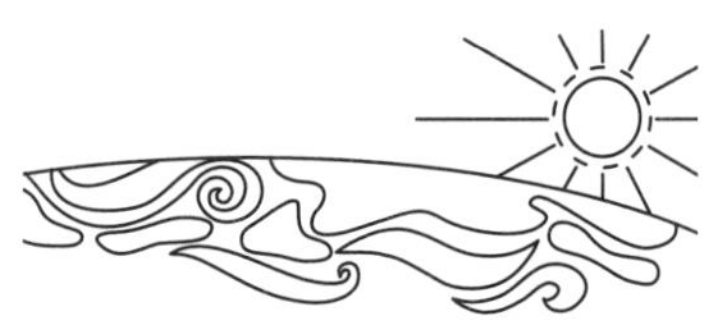

Copy the text. Remember to be careful with your diagonal joins.

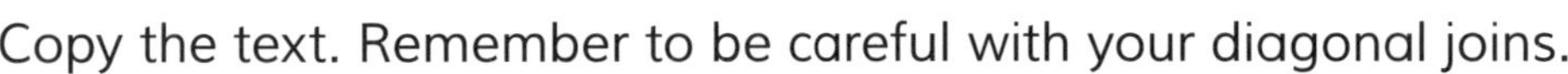

Today, we know that Earth is spherical, but there was a time when it was believed to be flat. Many early maps depict a flat Earth. From our everyday view, Earth looks flat. However, the view of our planet from a spacecraft gives us a more accurate idea of its true shape. Today, scientists analyse photographs taken from satellites in outer space, which enable us to see objects in space very clearly. An image with many pixels even allows astronomers to see tornadoes on the surface of other planets in great detail.

Self-assessment

Rate your diagonal joins.

I need more practice.

They're good.

They're excellent!

ISBN: 9780170424073

Touch joins

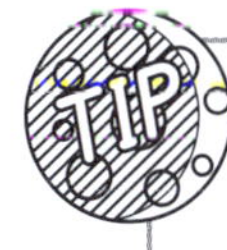

Remember: joining diagonally to a, c, d, g and q requires a touch join. Make a high exit, then lift your pen and drop in the next letter.

Copy these words with touch joins. The dots show where the touch joins are.

planets galaxy magnetic metallic mantle aqua

heat rotate clouds degrees volcanoes asteroids

rotational terrestrial eclipse launch accelerate

wavelength equator descent weather equal radiation

Copy the text, then add dots to indicate where there would be touch joins in cursive.

astronaut lunar starlight meteoroid waxing

magnitude black hole elliptical mass radiation

A waxing moon is a phase of the lunar cycle.

Prove your dots were placed correctly by writing the text in cursive.

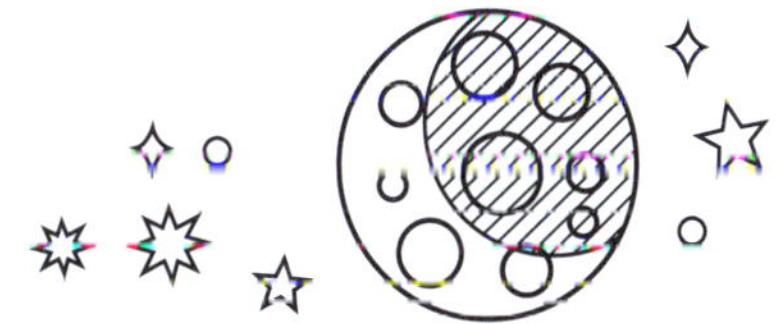

ISBN: 9780170424073

Using touch joins when joining diagonally to a, c, d, g and q will help you to write more fluently by reducing the amount you need to retrace.

Use a pen lift for touch joins and after a capital letter. You can also use a pen lift to help you move your hand comfortably across the page as you write.

Rewrite the text in cursive. Be careful with your touch joins and pen lifts.

Imagine living and working in a space station! Astronauts stay in space for months at a time, and are busy doing things like conducting experiments and repairing parts of the space station. Astronauts need to exercise for at least two hours a day because the lack of gravity wastes away muscles and weakens bones. Space station exercise equipment is different from that on Earth. Astronauts use specially designed space treadmills, stationary bikes and weightlift stations.

ISBN: 9780170424073

Self-assessment: Touch joins

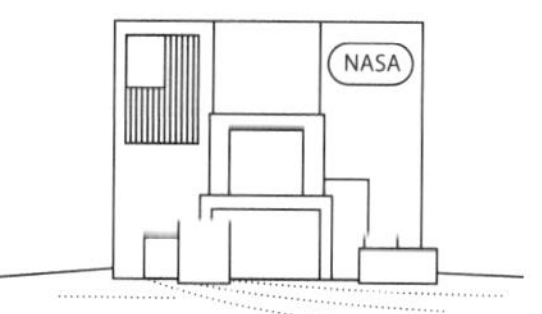

Copy the text. Remember to be careful with your touch joins.

The Hubble Space Telescope flies above Earth's atmosphere, taking digital photographs that show the position of the clusters of stars in space. It takes photographs of planets, stars and galaxies, and sends them back to Earth through radio waves. NASA launched the telescope from the Kennedy Space Center, Florida, USA, in 1990. The Hubble Space Telescope orbits Earth at a speed of over 27 000 kilometres per hour.

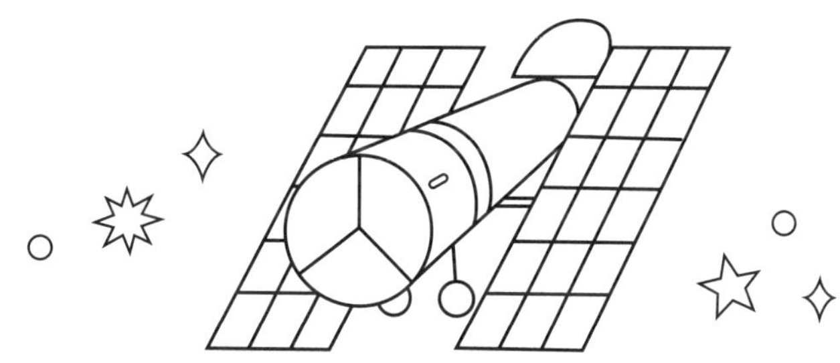

Self-assessment

Rate your touch joins.

- [ ] They're good.
- [ ] They're very good.
- [ ] They're excellent!

ISBN: 9780170424073

Horizontal joins

bu oz ru

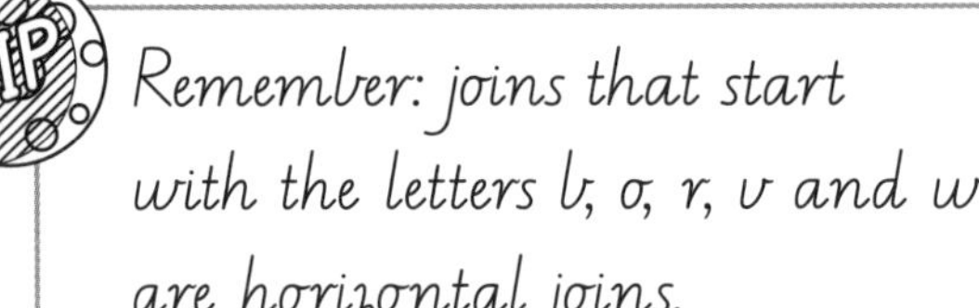

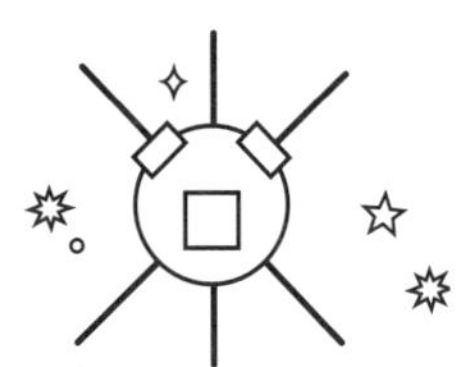

Vanguard 1 satellite

Copy these letter pairs with horizontal joins.

bi bu by vi vu vy oi oj

om on op or ou ov oy oz

ri rp rr ru wi wm wn wp

Copy these words with horizontal joins.

ozone morph biomaterial binocular envy

snowy abyss voyage uninhabited savvy

turbojet project electromagnetic automatic

thermometer convoy equilibrium experiment

surprise windstorm viewpoint tomorrow

Copy the sentence three times. Be careful with your horizontal joins.

Earth's ozone layer protects us and makes Earth habitable.

ISBN: 9780170424073

Horizontal joins to anti-clockwise letters

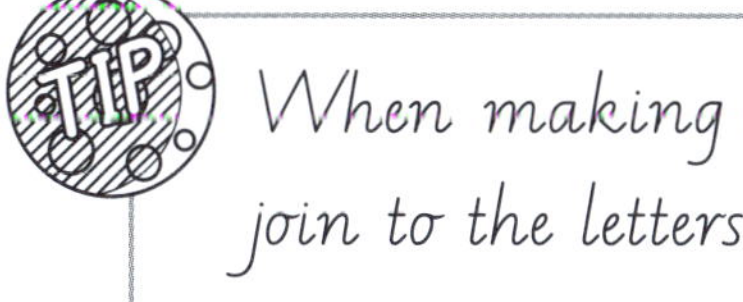

When making a horizontal join to the letters a, c, d, g or o, some retracing is required.

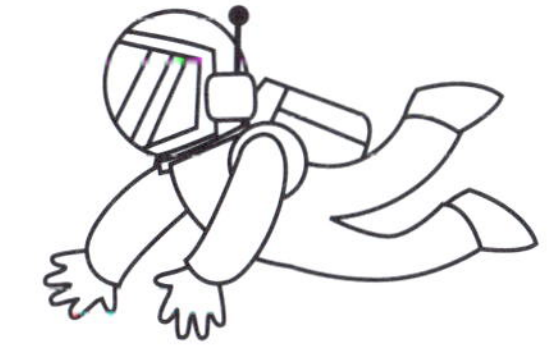

Copy these letter pairs with horizontal joins to anti-clockwise letters.

ba bo oa oc od og oo ra

rc rd ro va vo wa wd wo

Copy these words with horizontal joins to anti-clockwise letters.

rocket moon vacuum water Armstrong base radio

wavelength Sea of Tranquillity astronaut dog module

Copy this story starter, being careful with your horizontal joins. Continue the story, using as many words with horizontal joins from b, o, r, v and w as possible.

On 16 July 1969, the American astronaut Neil Armstrong

ISBN: 9780170424073

Horizontal joins to 'e'

Remember: dip a little lower when making a horizontal join to 'e'.

lower dip

be oe re ve we

Copy these words, then underline letter pairs with a horizontal join to 'e'.

discovered three very travel pressure coexist

extreme nowhere best powerful adventurer

current drive over observed active explore

Rewrite these words in cursive to practise your horizontal joins to 'e'.

region benefit arrived several atmosphere

hemisphere structure interest average echoes

Copy the text. Remember to be careful with your horizontal joins to 'e'.

Jupiter is very large. It is the largest planet in the solar system. Its stripes are actually clouds made up of ammonia and water. Astronomers believe it has over 60 moons. Jupiter does not have a solid surface because it is made up of swirling gases and liquid.

ISBN 9780170424073

Horizontal joins and speed loops

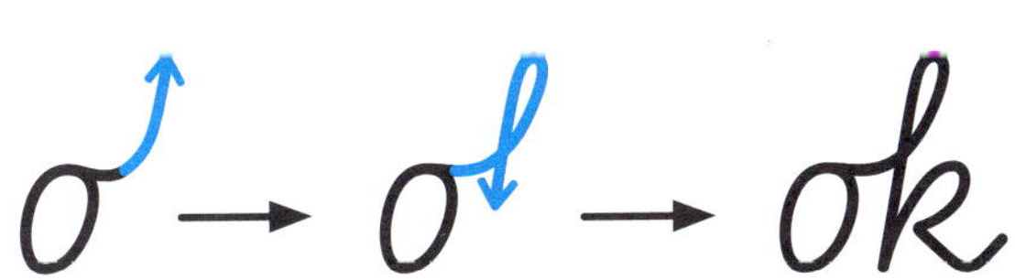

Make a smooth upsweeping join before looping to the ascender. The loop crosses at the height of a body letter.

Copy these letter pairs.

bb bh bl ob oh ok ol rb

rh rk rl wb wh wk wl vl

Practise speed loops from horizontal joins. Copy the words.

global technology objective whole revolve work

solar turbulence violence volcanic pavlova

obscure observatory whirl starlight absolute

lift off able black blast collide probe

Remember: when joining horizontally to the letter 'f', continue the exit of the letter before and form a loop. Use the crossbar to join to the next letter.

Copy these words with horizontal joins to 'f'.

dwarf planet surf snowflake offer often

imperfect butterfly officer profit professional

ISBN: 9780170424073

Horizontal joins to 's'

Use a horizontal join from b, o, r, v and w to the letter 's'. Make a careful horizontal sweep, then retrace the top part of 's' before completing the letter.

rs

Remember: when joining horizontally to 's', the shape of the 's' doesn't change.

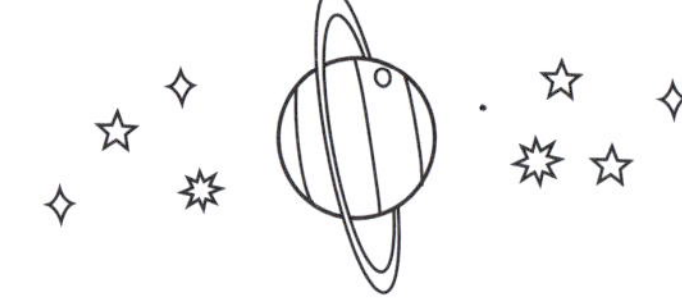

Copy these letter pairs with horizontal joins to 's'.

bs os rs vs ws bs os rs vs ws

bs os rs vs ws bs os rs vs ws

Copy the text, being careful with your horizontal joins to 's'.

Mars appears close doors post most

oscillate observe cosmic expose position

abstract gears torsion windows purpose

officers atmosphere sparse thermostat

shows interstellar years crews arrows

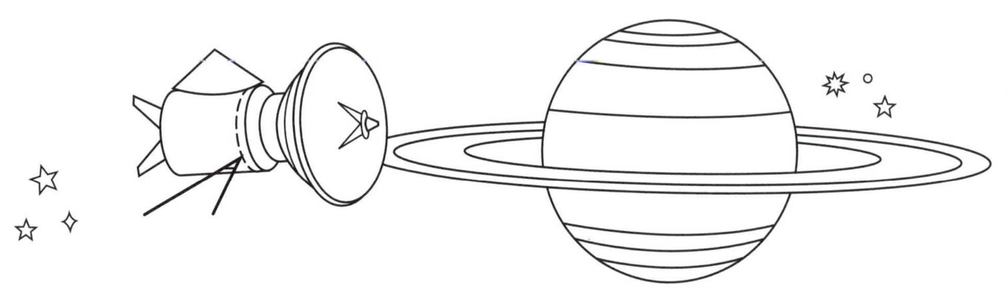

ISBN: 9780170424073

Horizontal joins from 'f'

Use the crossbar to join from 'f'.

Copy these words.

fascinating familiar fantasy fiction

fire future fuselage fluorescent flame

Lower the crossbar to join from 'f' to 'e'.

Copy these words.

feature fellowship fearsome fearless

few feud feeling fend feast

Remember to retrace when joining from 'f' to 'o'.

Copy these words.

fortunate forgive forceful forecast

Copy this tongue twister. Be careful with your horizontal joins from 'f'.

Our favourite futuristic fantasy films feature fatal feuds between formidable family members.

ISBN: 9780170424073

Horizontal joins review

Take a letter from each box to make letter pairs with horizontal joins.

oc

b f o r v w	to	a b c d e g h i k l m n o p r s t u x y z

Copy these words, then underline the horizontal joins.

clothes astronaut formal outside move rocket

around protects dangers several ways vacuum

oxygen water sound dangerous moving orbit

carbon possible cooling during primary world

bang observable force buffer research transport

Make new words by adding a letter or letters to these word endings with horizontal joins.

______oat ______og ______orn ______ood ______ook

______ork ______oon ______one ______ost ______oor

get.ga/PMWA184

ISBN: 9780170424073

Self-assessment: Horizontal joins

Copy the text. Remember to be careful with your horizontal joins.

Jupiter is the fifth planet from the Sun and the largest planet in our solar system. It is a gas giant, and may appear to be hazy when viewed from an observatory. Four large, luminous moons move in orbit around Jupiter, along with many other smaller moons. This amazing planet broadcasts radio waves strong enough for scientific equipment on Earth to detect.

ISBN: 9780170424073

Slope

How consistent is your slope? Trace and copy these words within the wavy lines, then use a ruler to draw slope lines along the vertical parts of the letters.

Copy the words, using the slope lines as a guide.

dust storms iron oxide polar ice caps planet

rings orbit scorching surface hydrogen helium

ISBN: 9780170424073

Spacing

Read the sentence, then rewrite it with even spacing between letters and words.

Consistent spac ing betw een le tters an d

word s makes yo u r handwriting eas ier to r ead.

Write each word in the word shapes. If your letter spacing is even, the word will fit in the shape.

dwarf temperature comets

surface distance asteroids

Neptune Saturn Jupiter

Copy the text, then check your spacing. Colour a small square between each word.

When the solar system was formed, the leftover material

became asteroids, meteoroids and comets. These orbit the

Sun. A meteor, or shooting star, is a meteoroid that enters

Earth's atmosphere and burns up in a blaze of light.

ISBN: 9780170424073

Size

Copy these words in the spaces provided. How much does your handwriting vary in size from the models?

speeds travel gravity energy temperature

atmosphere galaxy moons satellites particles

spiral debris spacecraft formation motion

Sometimes you need to write at a different size. Can you change the size of your writing and maintain your legibility?

space space space space

Write the word 'Mars' in cursive in the word shapes. Use the shapes to help you write at a consistent size.

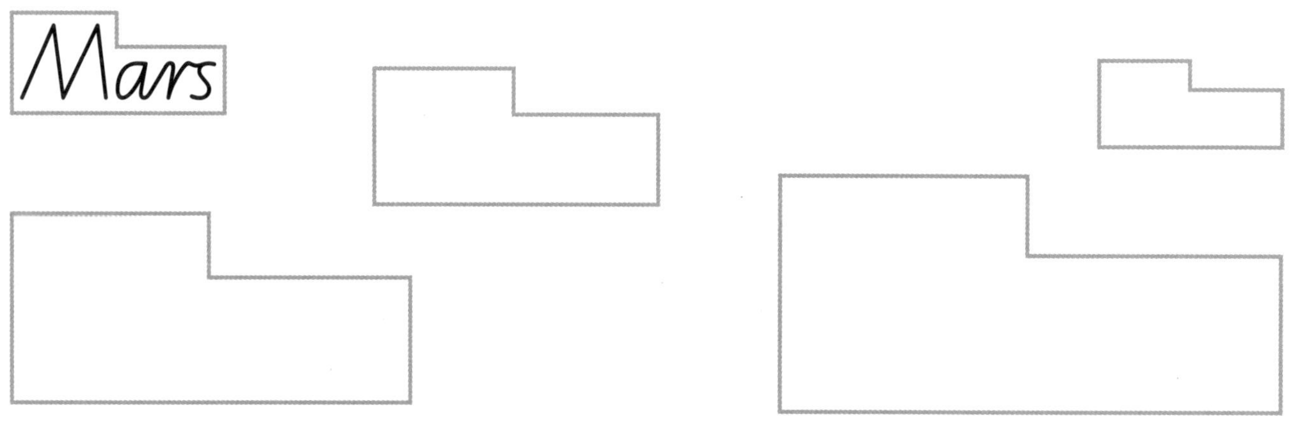

ISBN: 9780170424073

Copy the text. Take special care with the slope, spacing and size of your letters.

Saturn, like the other gas giants, Jupiter, Uranus and Neptune, is surrounded by rings. Saturn's rings are very bright and contain lots of material. The rings are actually made up of thousands of ringlets. The band of rings is up to 282 000 km across, but only 1 km thick. The dusty ice particles that make up the rings vary in size from grains to boulders. Scientists have been using the Hubble Space Telescope to learn more about the rings.

get.ga/PMWA185

Peer review

Ask your partner to give you some feedback on how well you wrote the text above. Ask them to notice how careful you were with your slope, spacing and size.

2 stars (two things you did well)

1 wish (a way for you to improve)

ISBN: 9780170424073

Introducing the print alphabet

The print alphabet can be used for labelling maps, charts, diagrams and graphs, for writing headings and for addressing envelopes.

m → m

In print script, most letters don't have exits or entries.

f → f

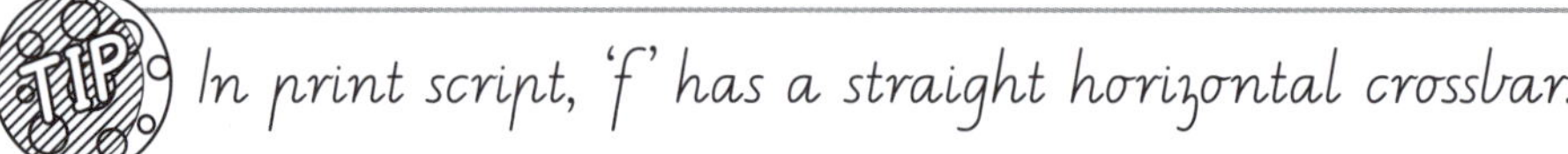

In print script, 'f' has a straight horizontal crossbar.

z → z

The letter 'z' has no tail.

Trace and copy the print alphabet.

a b c d e f g h i j k l m n o p q r s t u v w x y z

Can you label the planets of our solar system, beginning nearest to the Sun? Use print script.

The planets of our solar system

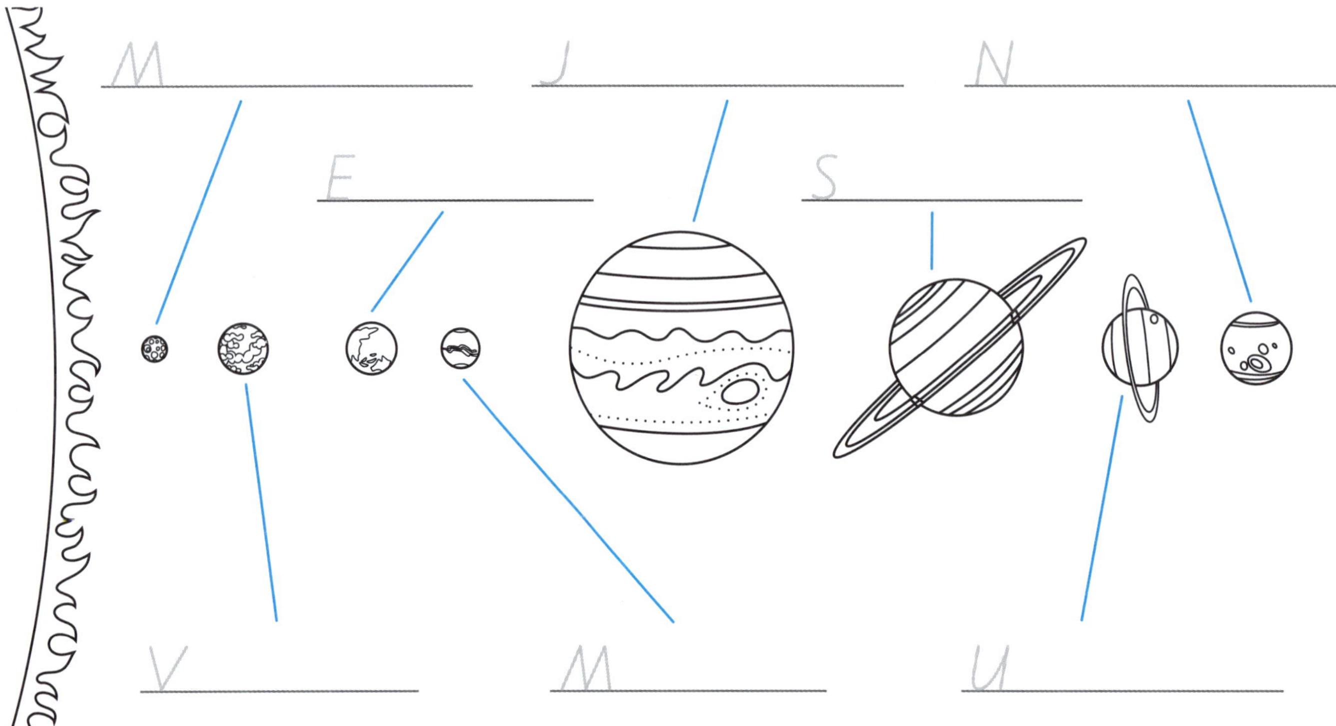

ISBN: 9780170424073

Label the parts of the spacesuit. Use print script. Give the diagram a suitable heading.

sun visor	backpack	temperature control valve
TV camera	in-suit drink bag	display control module
boots	coloured ID stripes	helmet gloves

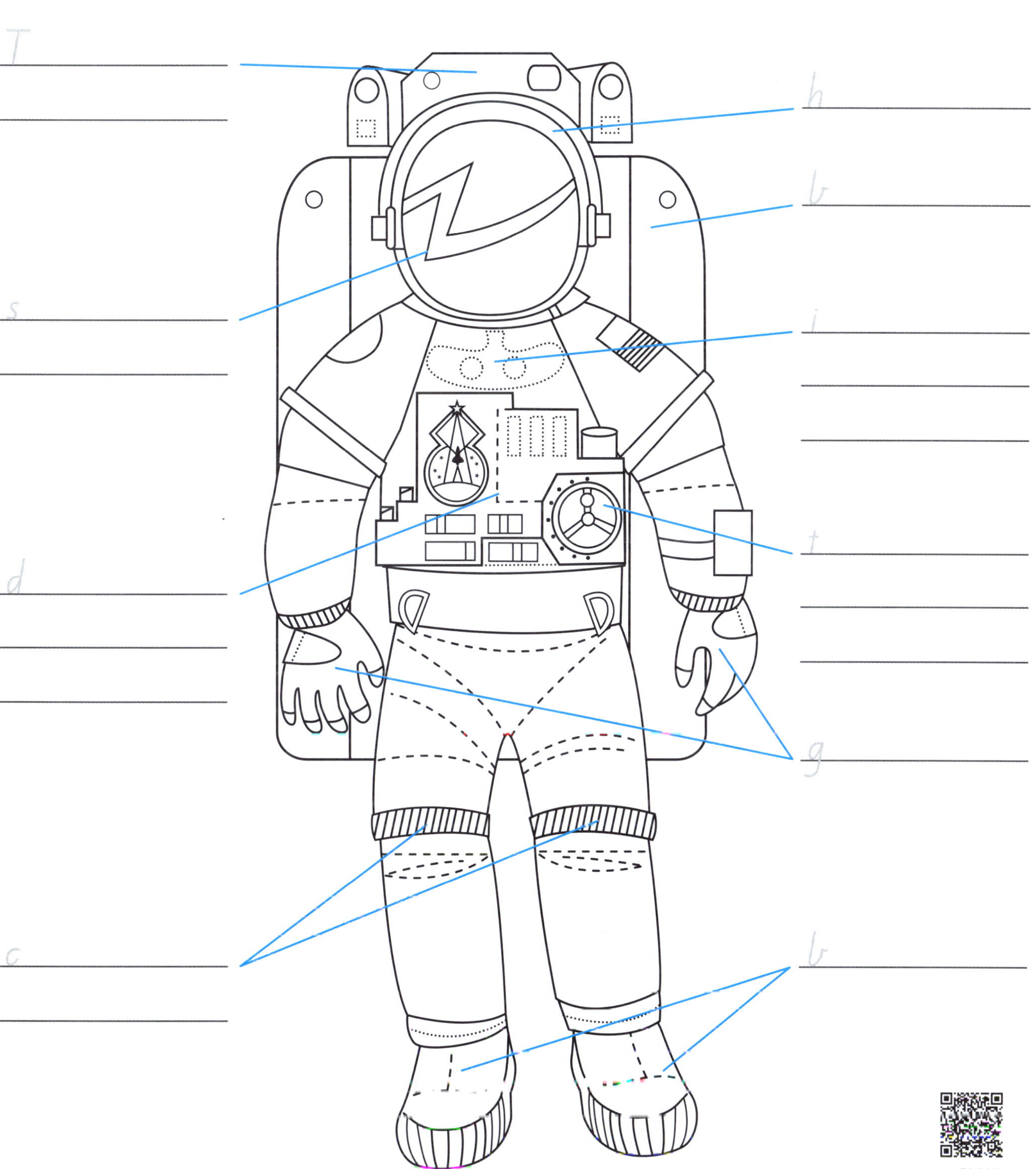

get.gg/PMWA186

ISBN: 9780170424073

Unjoined letters

Revise your unjoined letters.

a b c d e f g h i j k l m n o p q r s t u v w x y z

Copy these words.

Ceres dwarf planet asteroid belt inner craters

Use the words above to complete the sentences. Then copy the text.

Ceres is a ______ ______. It is located in the ______ ______

between Mars and Jupiter. ______ is covered in many small

______. It is the only dwarf planet in the ______ solar system.

Copy the facts about dwarf planets.

Dwarf planets are smaller than planets.

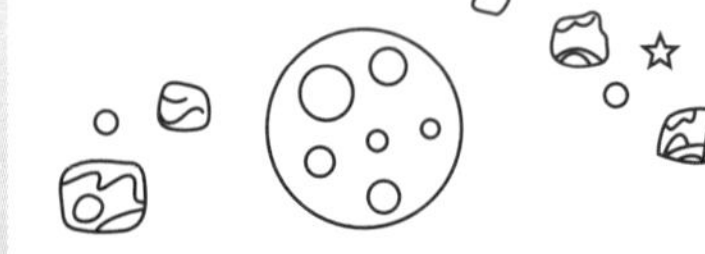

They are rounded objects that orbit the Sun.

Some dwarf planets have moons of their own.

Pluto is now called a dwarf planet, instead of a planet.

ISBN: 9780170424073

Capital letters

Revise your capital letters.

A B C D E F G H I J K L M N O P

Q R S T U V W X Y Z

Rewrite these words in all capital letters.

living	working	space	food	clothing
exercise	communicate	research	zero gravity	
self-care	daily	mission	dreams	snoring
excitement	motion	nightmares	wake	hours

List the capital letters in the words you have written above that have downstrokes.

List the capital letters in the words you have written above that have a rounded shape.

List the capital letters in the words you have written above that have diagonal lines.

ISBN: 9780170424073

Numerals

Add the missing numerals and numeral names to the table.

Planet	Diameter	Diameter in words
Mercury	4879 km	Four thousand, eight hundred and seventy nine kilometres
Venus		Twelve thousand, one hundred and four kilometres
Earth	12 756 km	
Mars		Six thousand, seven hundred and ninety-two kilometres
Jupiter		One hundred and forty-two thousand, nine hundred and eighty-four kilometres
Saturn	120 536 km	
Uranus	51 118 km	
Neptune		Forty-nine thousand, five hundred and twenty-eight kilometres

Which planet has the largest diameter? ______________________

Which planet has the smallest diameter? ______________________

Which planet is most similar in size to Earth? ______________________

List the planets from smallest to largest. ______________________

____

ISBN: 9780170424073

Punctuation

Rewrite these jokes. Include question marks where necessary.

Q: When do astronauts eat their sandwiches

A: At launch time!

Q: What kind of music can you hear in space

A: A Nep-tune.

Rewrite the text in cursive. Include quotation marks, and give each speaker a new line.

Do you think you will be famous when you grow up? the teacher asked her 10-year-old student. I don't know, but I do want to learn to fly, replied Neil Armstrong.

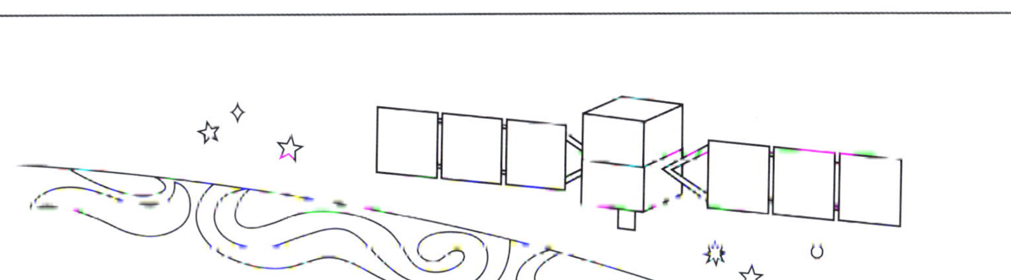

ISBN: 9780170424073

Double letter combinations

oss — double 's' from a horizontal join

ess — double 's' from a diagonal join

TIP: Remember: when double 's' comes after a horizontal join, modify the second 's'. When double 's' comes after a diagonal join, both letters are modified.

Copy these words with double 's'.

discussion mass pressure compress across

airless crosscheck dispossess boundless formless

ff

When writing double 'f', extend the crossbar of the first 'f' upwards to make a loop for the second 'f'. Lift your pen before adding each crossbar.

Copy the words with double 'f'.

difficult fluffy sufficient offline staff

offering offshore efficient graffiti giraffe

Copy these words with other double letter pairs.

moon books afternoon woollen occur feet

preen trees wheelbarrow aggravate buggy

shaggy bigger small taller skill cramming

symmetry dimmer thinner running sunny

chopping ripped currency furry hitting flatten

Rewrite these sentences, adding interesting adjectives where you can.
Remember to be careful with your double letter pairs.

The lunar buggy drove well across the surface of the Moon.

All the stars twinkled in the glittering sky.

The comet appeared to be dimmer than when it was last seen.

Only the thinnest crescent of the Moon appeared at night.

Walking in zero gravity can feel a bit like hopping.

The space shuttle lifted off right on time.

Astronauts are chosen from the fittest candidates.

ISBN: 9780170424073

Classifying joins

Sort these letter pairs into their correct join type.
Some letter pairs belong in more than one category.

cc ki ow wl vo ng rl co ac rs
ew wh ot cq om il nd ol cr on

Diagonal joins	Touch joins

Horizontal joins	Horizontal joins to speed loops

Rewrite this sentence in cursive five times.

The five boxing wizards jumped over the lazy frog.

List the letter pairs from the sentence above that join diagonally.

List the letter pairs from the sentence above that join horizontally.

List the letter pairs from the sentence above with touch joins.

Converting between scripts

Complete the table to practise unjoined, cursive and capital letters.

Unjoined	Cursive	Capital letters
Milky Way	Milky Way	
		UNIVERSE
solar system		
	planets	
Mercury		
	Venus	
Mars		
	asteroids	
Kuiper belt		
	satellites	
meteoroid		
	Earth	

Match each definition to a word from the table above. Write the answers in your preferred script.

- the red planet made up of dense rock: ______________________
- the galaxy that contains our solar system: ______________________
- a belt of small bodies beyond Neptune: ______________________
- spacecraft or astronomical bodies in orbit: ______________________
- the only planet known to support human life: ______________________
- the planet closest to the Sun: ______________________

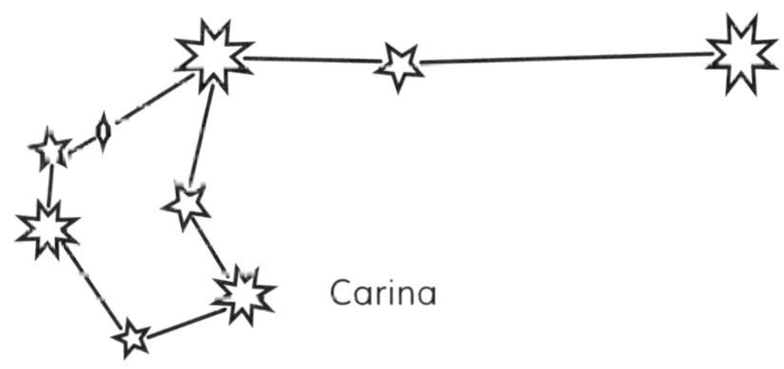

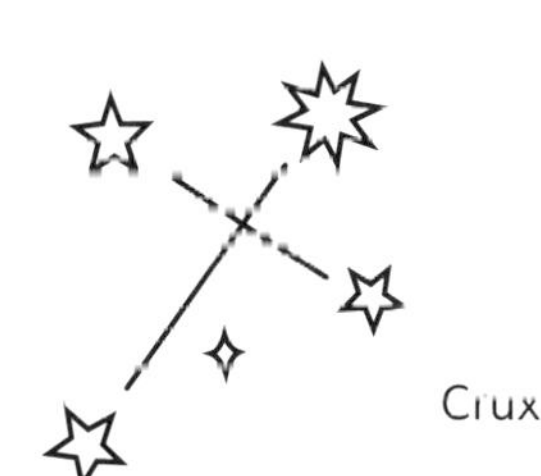

ISBN: 9780170424073

Labelling timelines with print script

get.ga/PMWA187

Add labels from the box to the timeline below. Use print script.

1969 First human on the Moon
1961 First human spaceflight
1971 First space probe to orbit Mars
1963 First woman in space
1957 First animal in orbit (Laika the dog)

A timeline of early space exploration

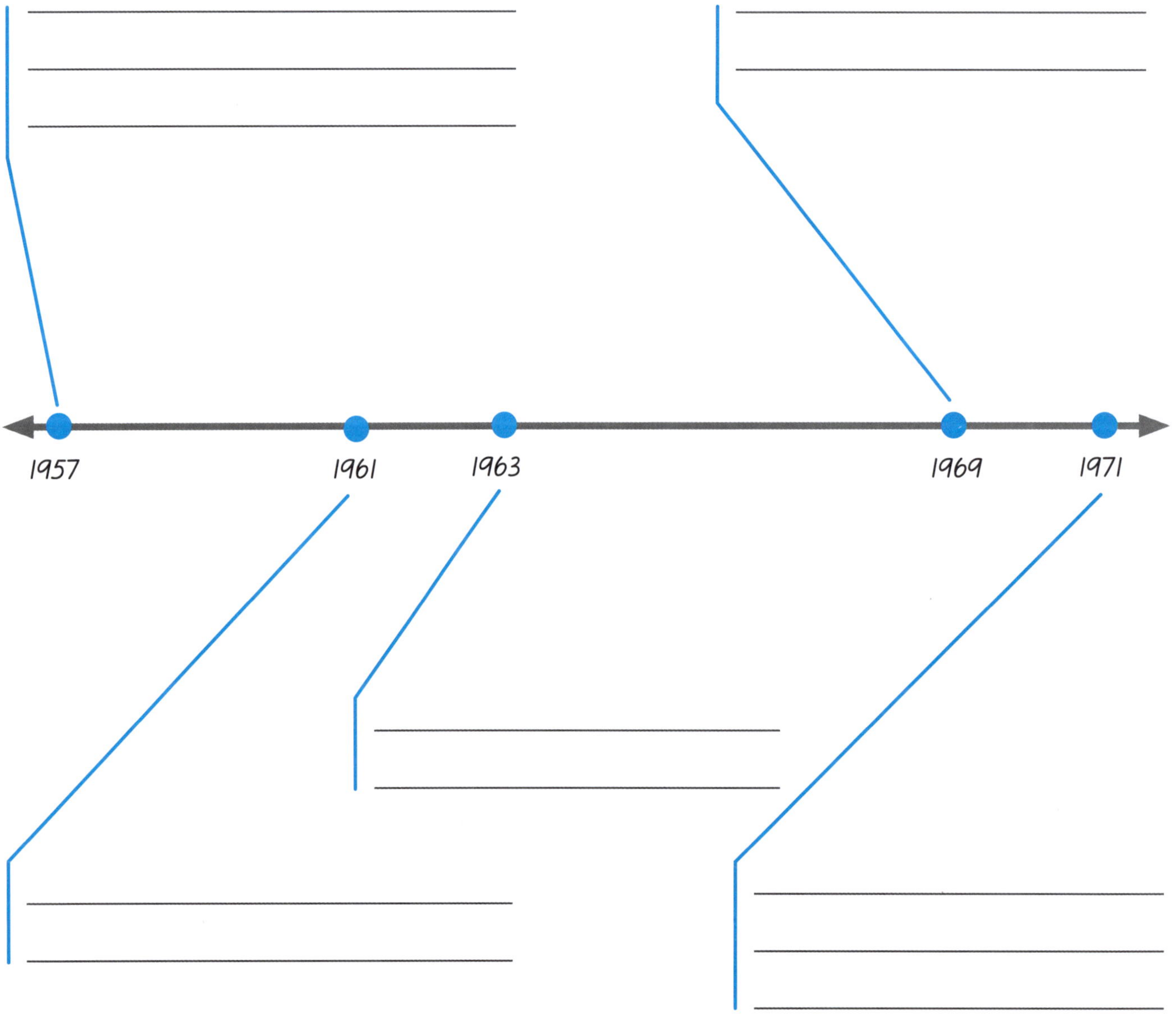

1957 1961 1963 1969 1971

Slope, spacing and size

Practise maintaining a consistent slope. Copy each word in the slope grid.

exoplanet

universe

terrestrial

atmosphere

habitable

telescope

Circle the statement or statements that apply to you.

- These slope grids were easy to use.
- These slope grids were hard to use.
- These slope grids helped me keep a consistent slope.

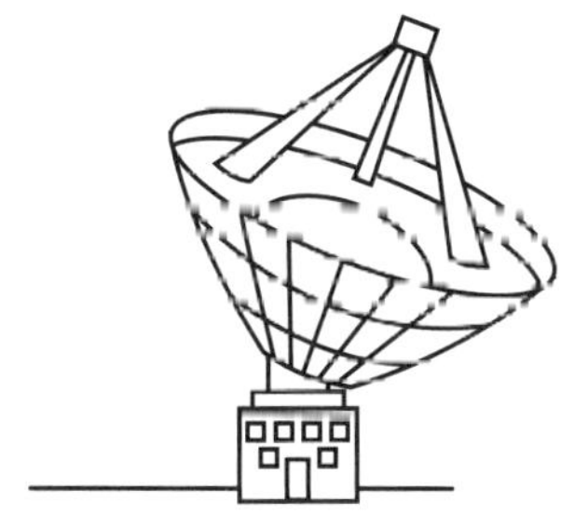

ISBN: 9780170424073

Copy the text, then check your spacing. Colour a small square between each word.

The second planet from the Sun is Venus. Its surface temperature is 472°C. The size of Venus is similar to that of Earth. Venus has no moons or rings, and it rotates in the opposite direction to most other planets.

Copy these patterns to practise maintaining even spacing between letters.

ooo www eee

uuu mmm ulul

Look at the different versions of the word 'Neptune'. Circle the version that has the most appropriate letter spacing.

Neptune Neptune Neptune Neptune

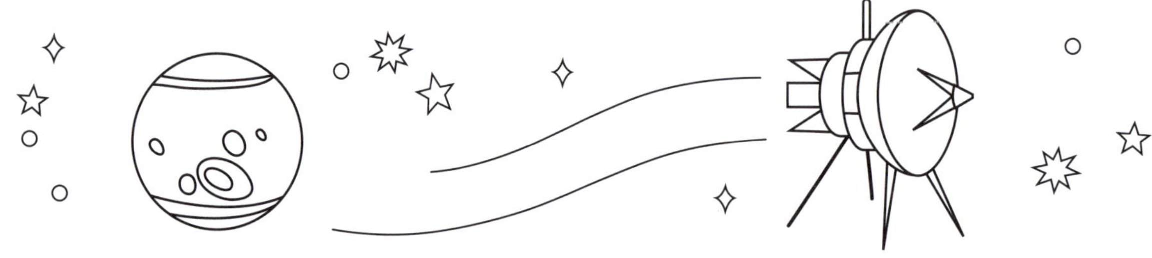

ISBN: 9780170424073

Trace and complete these patterns and words at different sizes. Try to maintain a consistent slope.

Speed and legibility

It is important to balance speed and accurate letter formation so your writing is quick and legible.

Work with a partner to find out how many times you can write the word 'eclipse' in cursive in one minute.

get.ga/PMWA188

eclipse ______________________________

______ times

Now write the word again. This time, write as neatly as you can. How many times did you write it in one minute?

eclipse ______________________________

______ times

Now find out how many times you can write the word neatly using unjoined writing in one minute.

eclipse ______________________________

______ times

My most legible script when writing at speed is: ____________________

Self-assessment: Legibility

Copy the text. Remember to be careful with your slope, spacing and size.

Scientists originally believed that Earth was flat, and there are many historical maps representing this. Indeed, sailors used to worry that when they reached the edge of the world, they would fall off! Once astronomers were able to look at photos of Earth taken from outer space, they saw that our planet has a round shape. This is because the force of gravity pulls all of Earth's mass towards its centre, which creates a sphere.

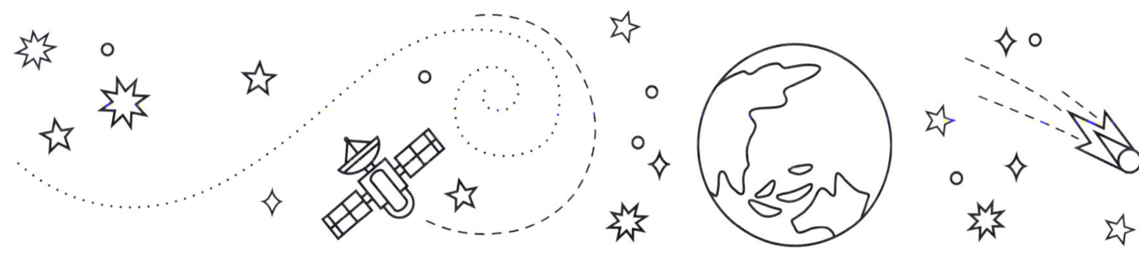

Self-assessment

Rate your slope, spacing and size.

They're inconsistent.

They're mostly consistent.

They're always consistent!

Handwriting in context

Draw a mind map that includes some outer space concepts covered in this book. You may use unjoined letters or cursive, but do your best to be as neat as possible, and to practise the handwriting skills you have learnt.

outer space

Independent writing activity

Imagine meeting Neil Armstrong after he became the first person to walk on the Moon. Write five questions you would like to ask him.

Imagine that all the planets in our solar system can support human life. Write a text explaining which planet you would like to visit and why.

Teacher observation guide

Student is: left-handed ☐ right-handed ☐

Student demonstrates correct posture, paper position and pencil grip. ☐

Student forms the letters of the Victorian Modern Cursive alphabet with accuracy. ☐

Student forms capital letters with accuracy. ☐

Student forms numerals with accuracy. ☐

Student forms the following joins with accuracy:

- speed loops ☐
- diagonal joins ☐
- touch joins ☐
- horizontal joins ☐

Student can convert between scripts. ☐

Student uses 9 mm regular writing lines with accuracy. ☐

Student has an understanding of the factors that influence legibility (slope, spacing, size, speed). ☐

Student can self-assess with accuracy. ☐

Student uses Victorian Modern Cursive confidently. ☐

Student is progressing towards a fluent and legible personal handwriting style. ☐

Notes:

....

....

....

Date:

....

CERTIFICATE

get.ga/PMWC180